SNOWFLAKE
MANDALAS

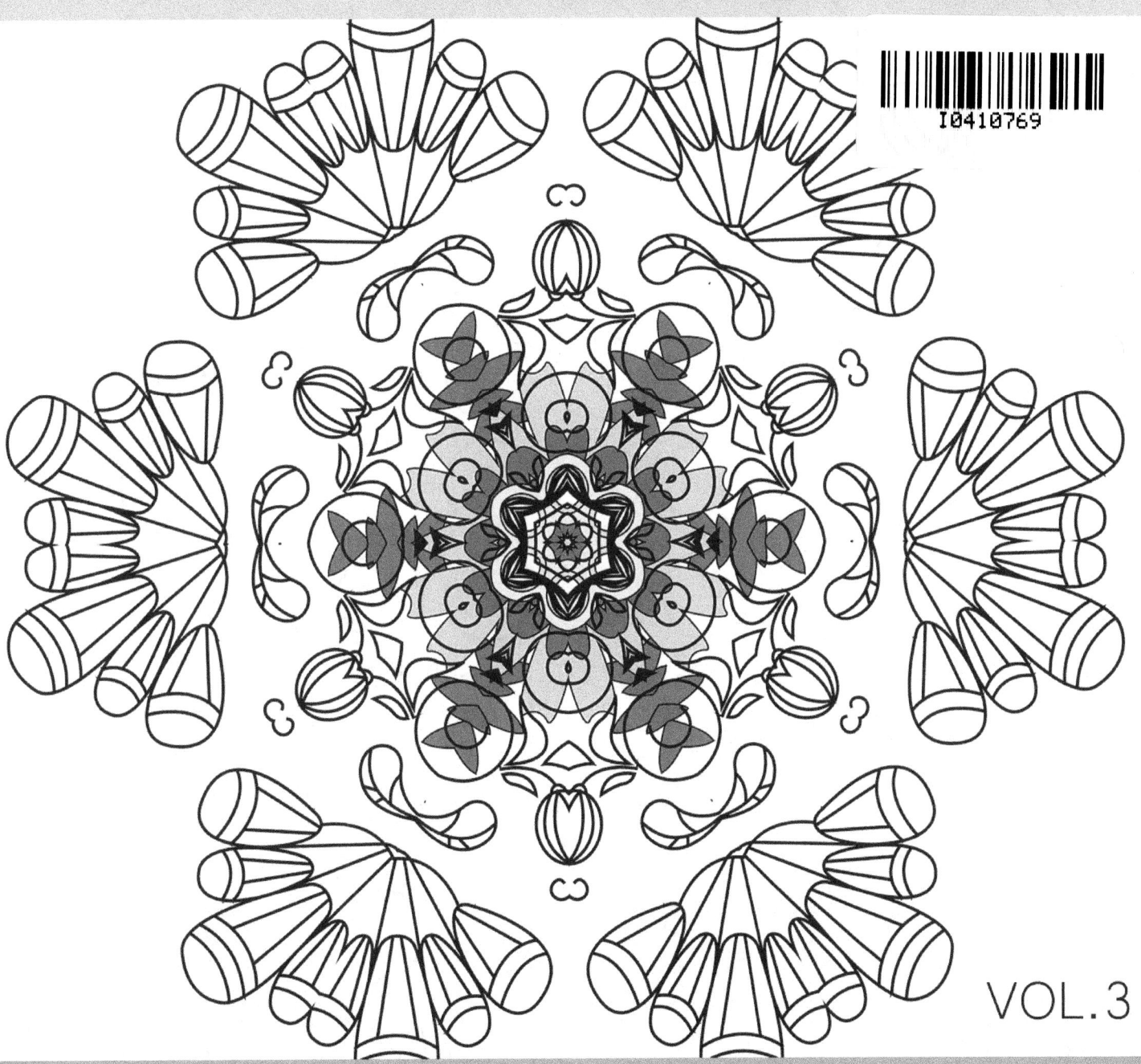

VOL.3

ADULT COLORING BOOK DESIGNS

COLOR TEST PAGE

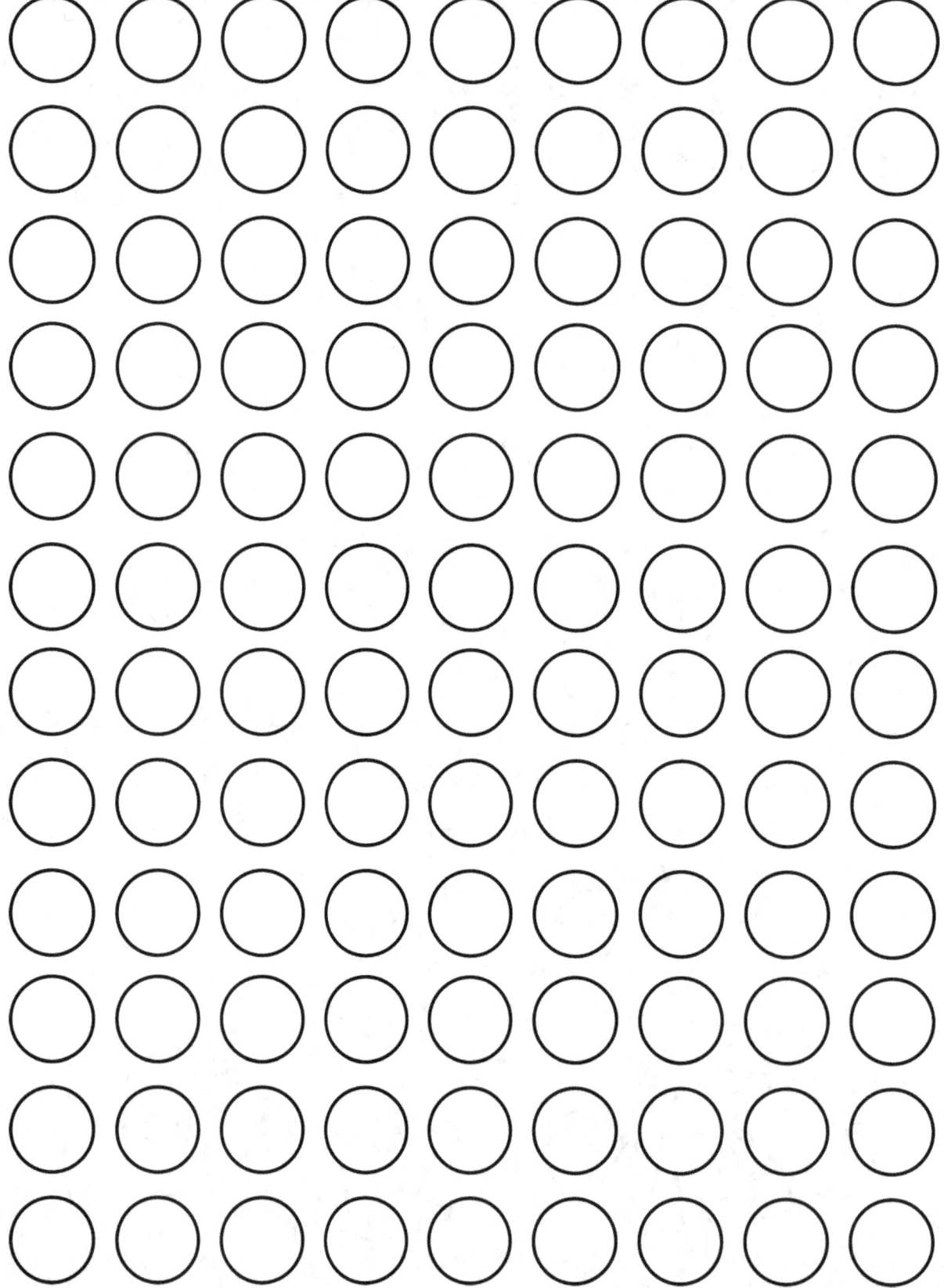

COLOR TEST PAGE

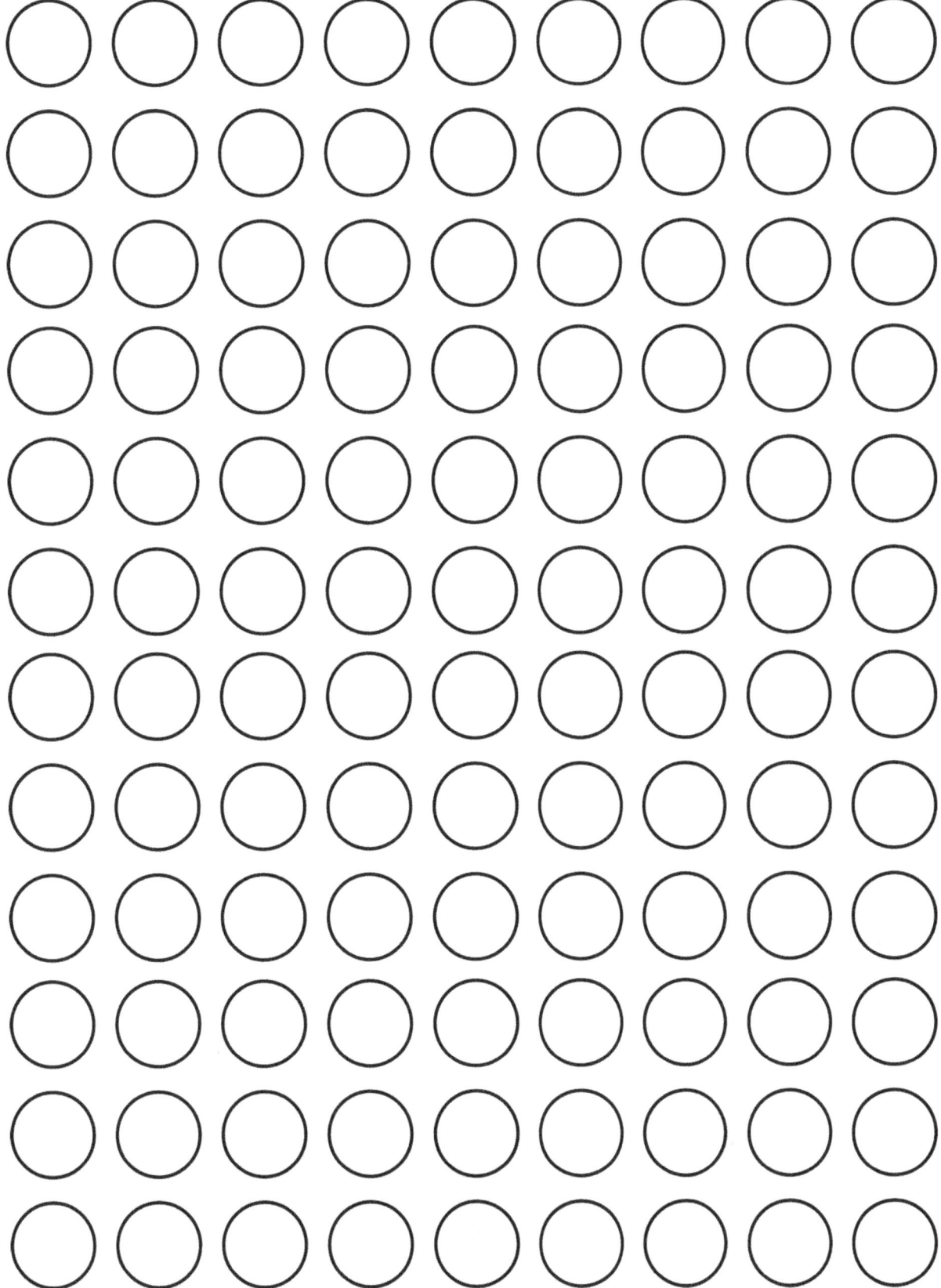

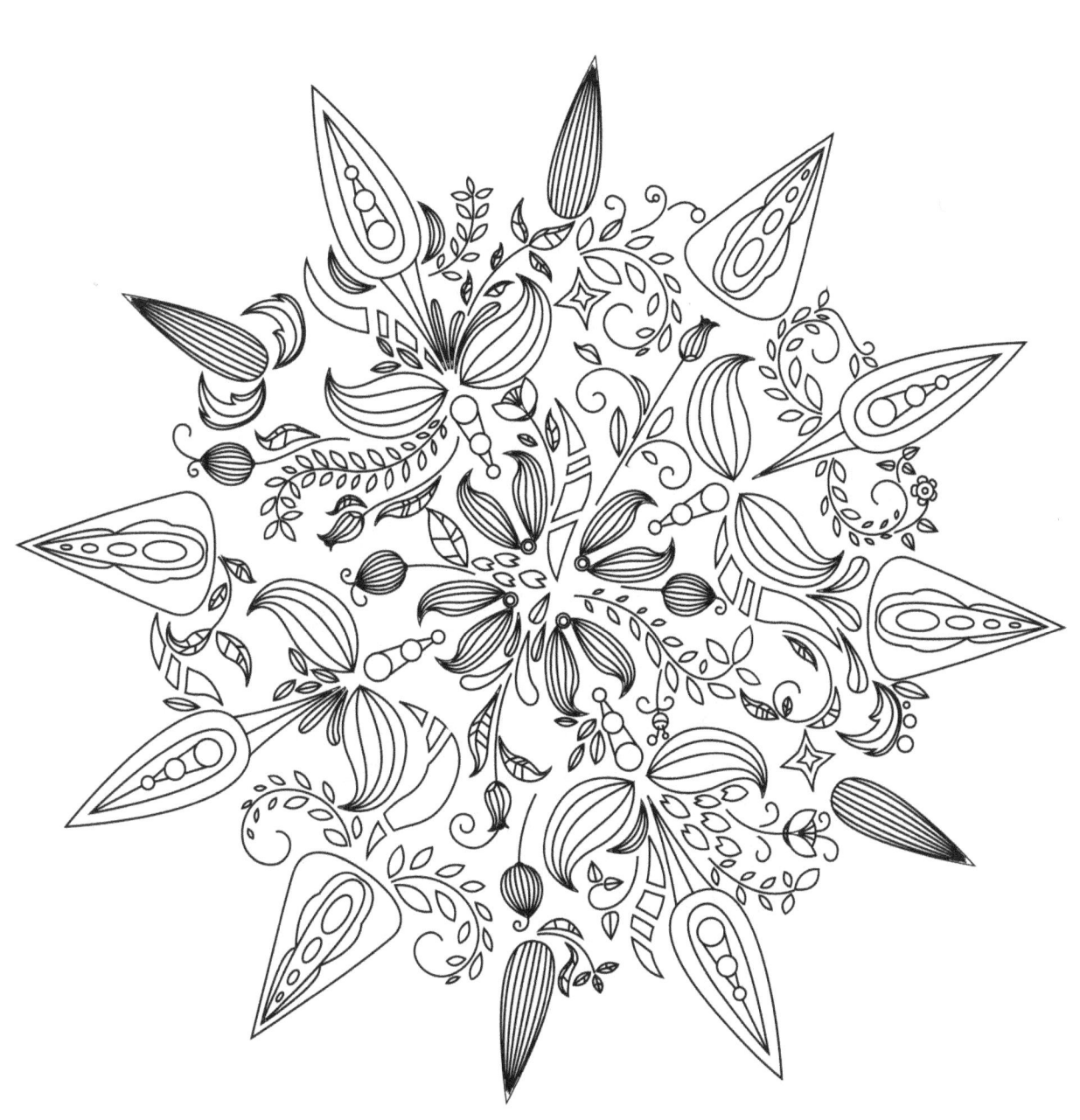

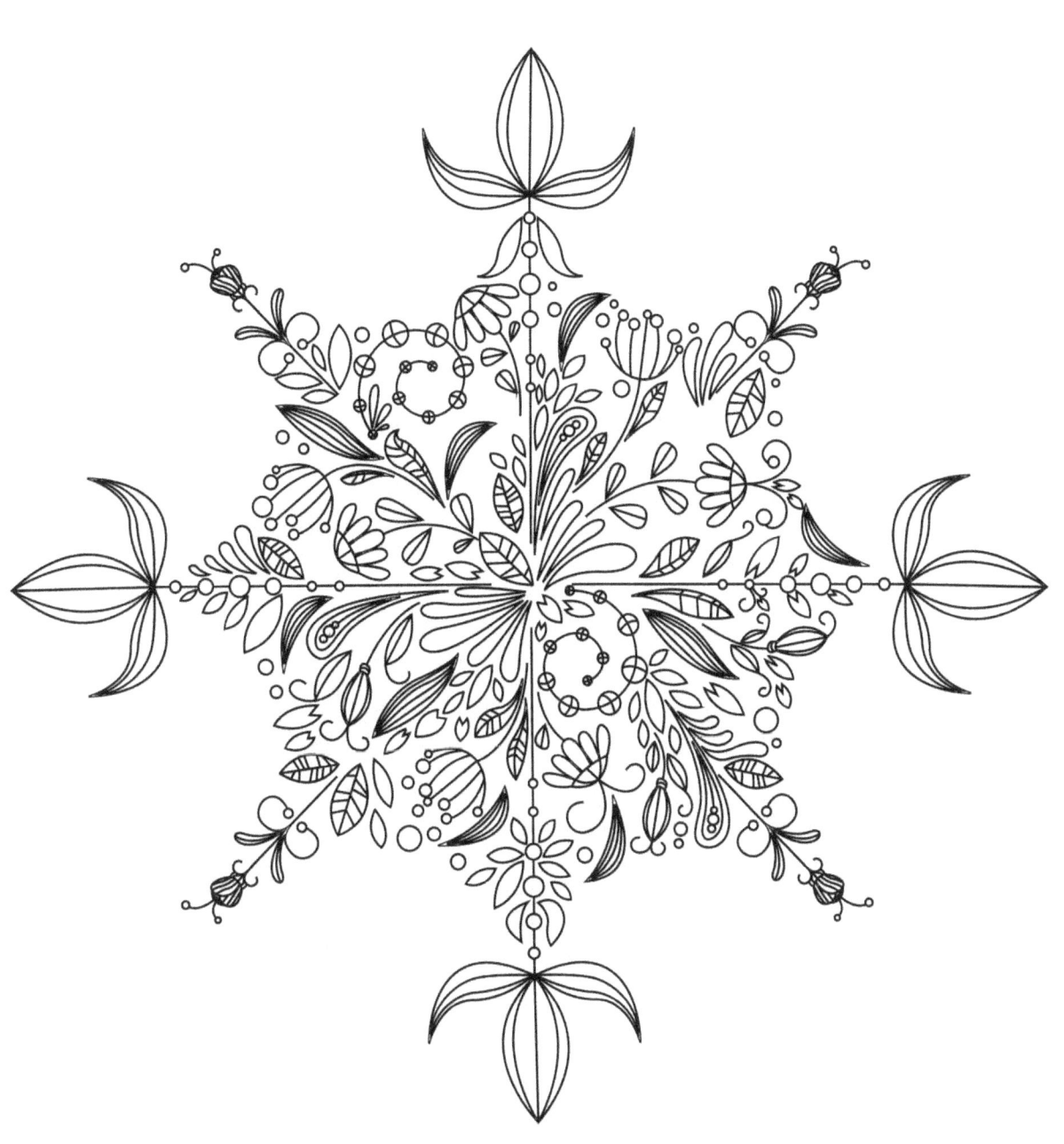

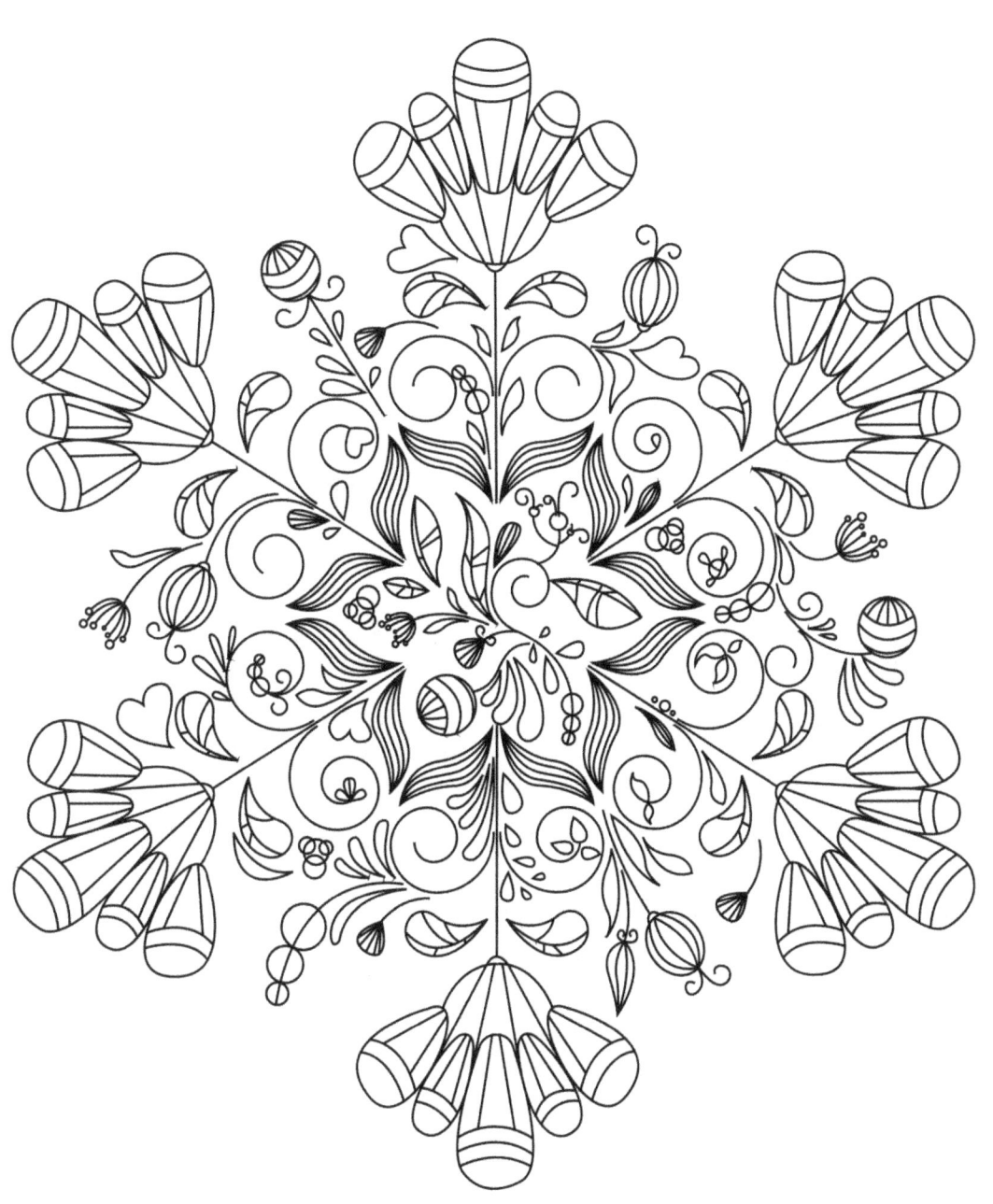

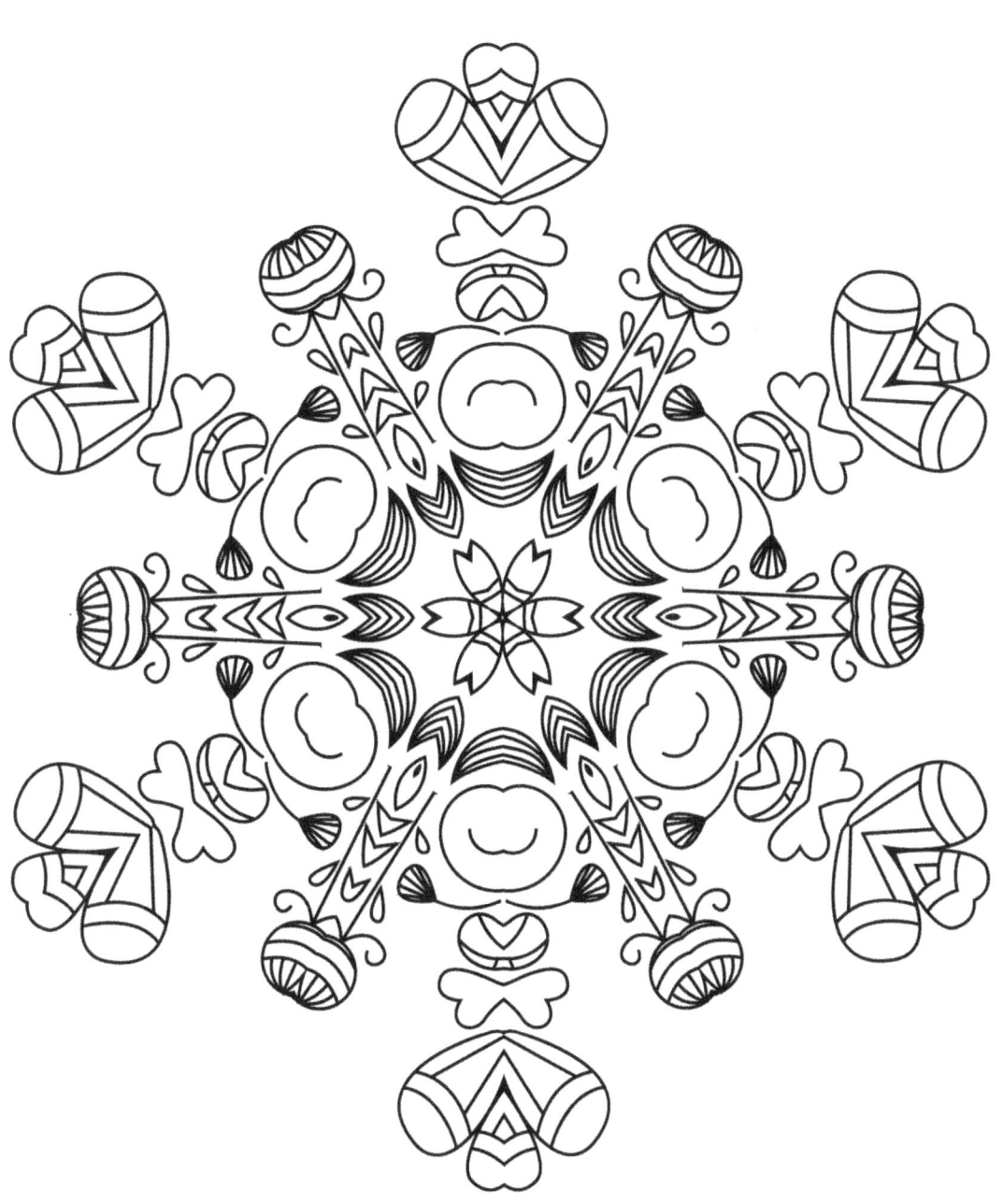

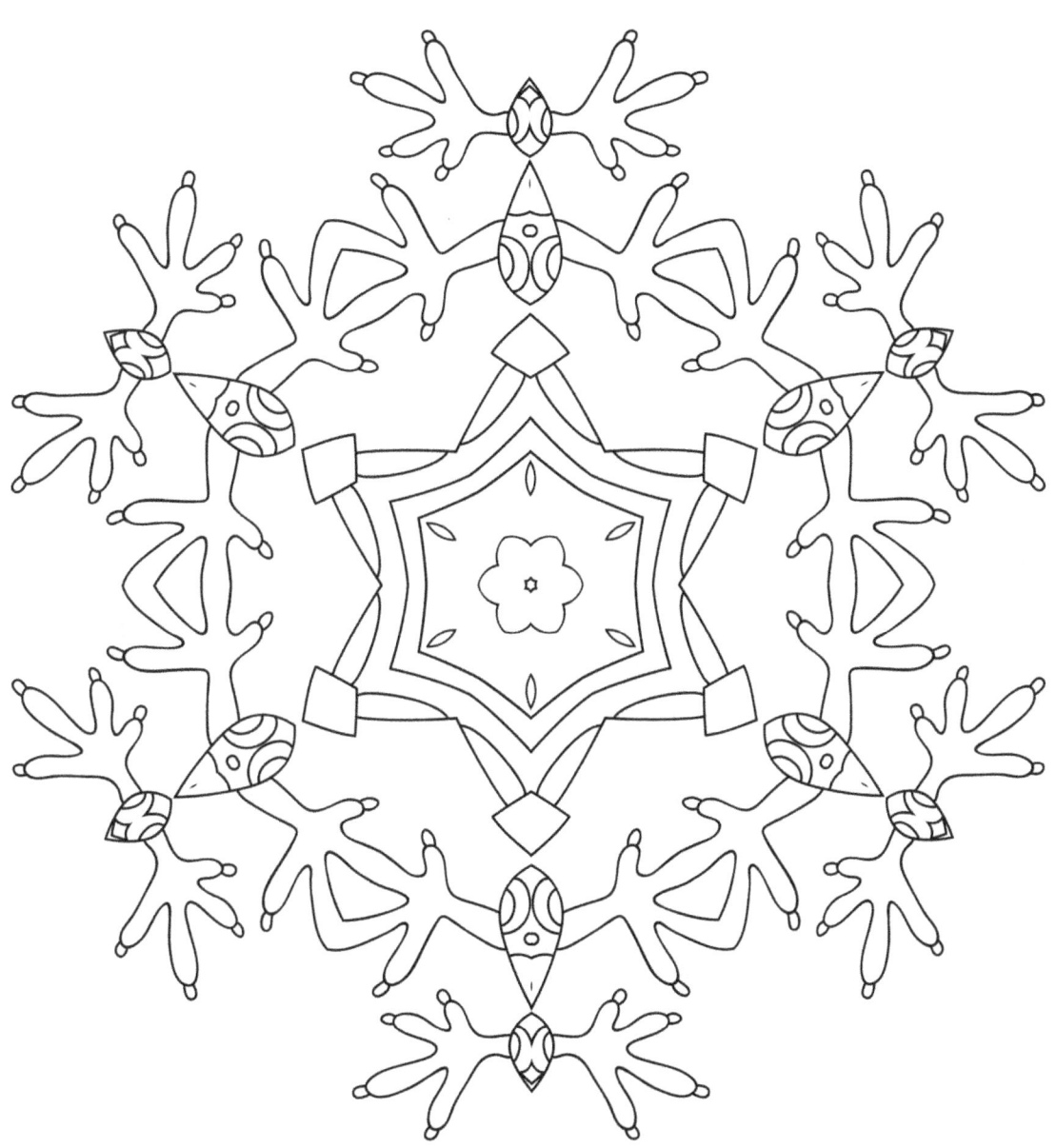

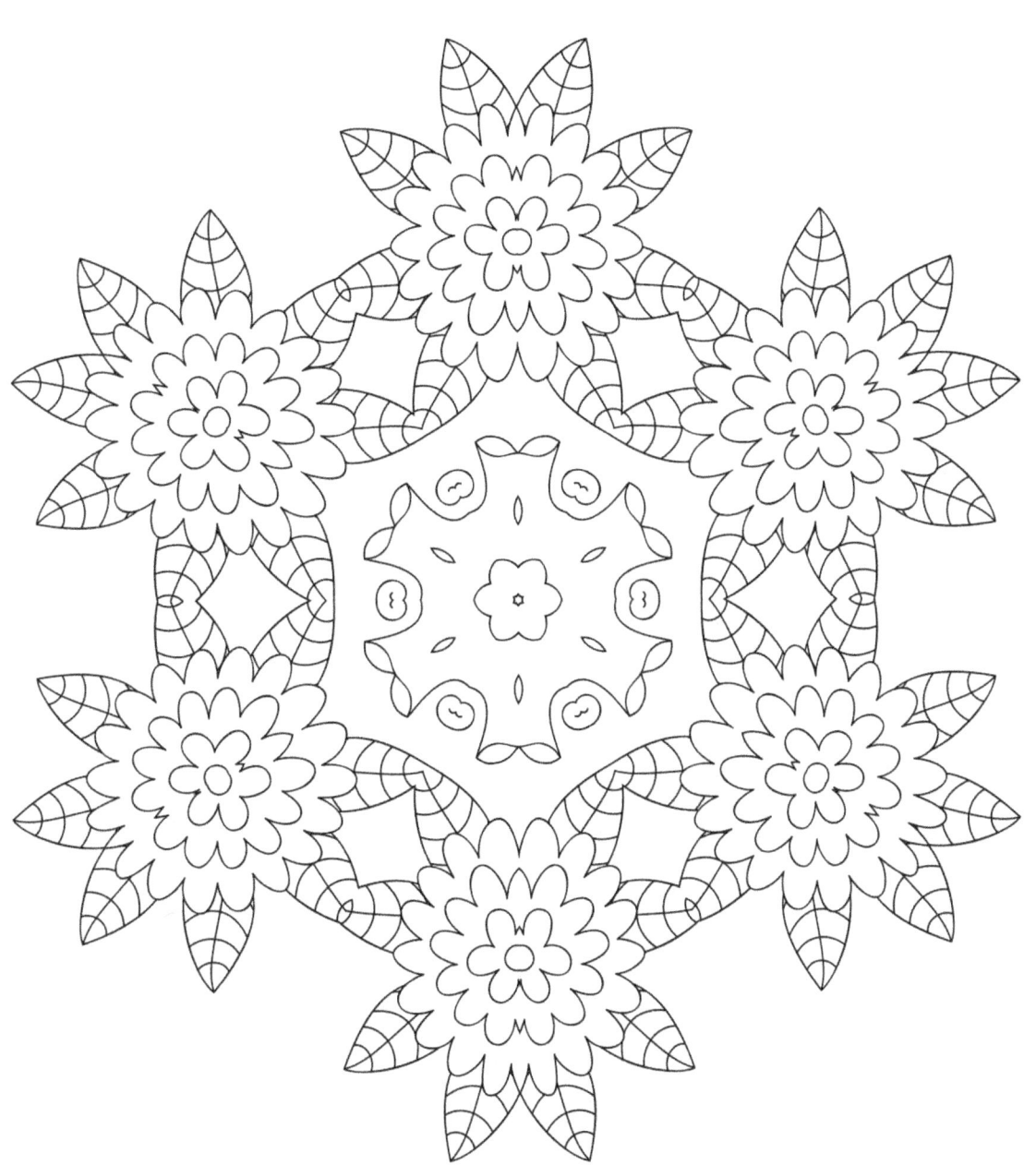

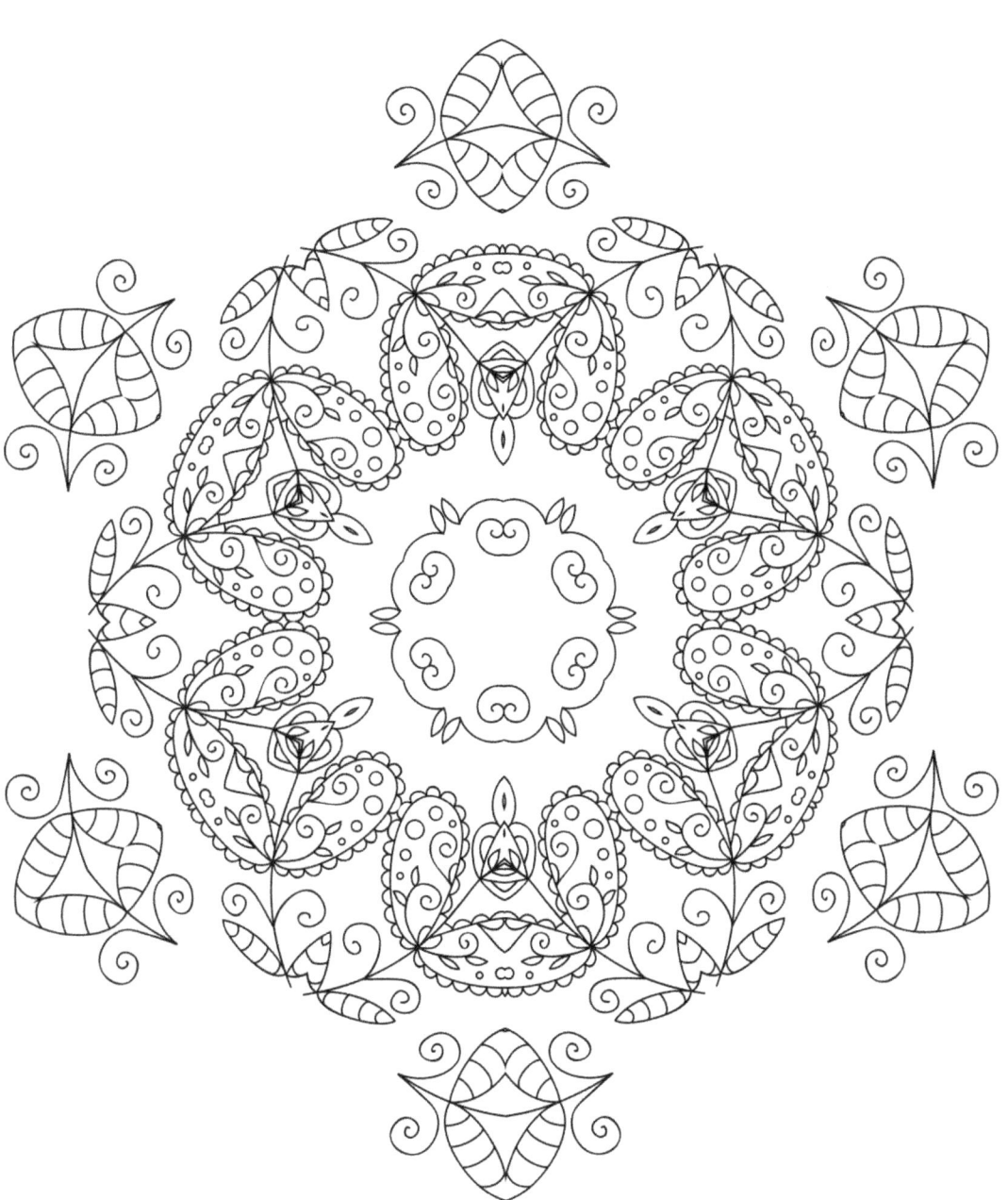

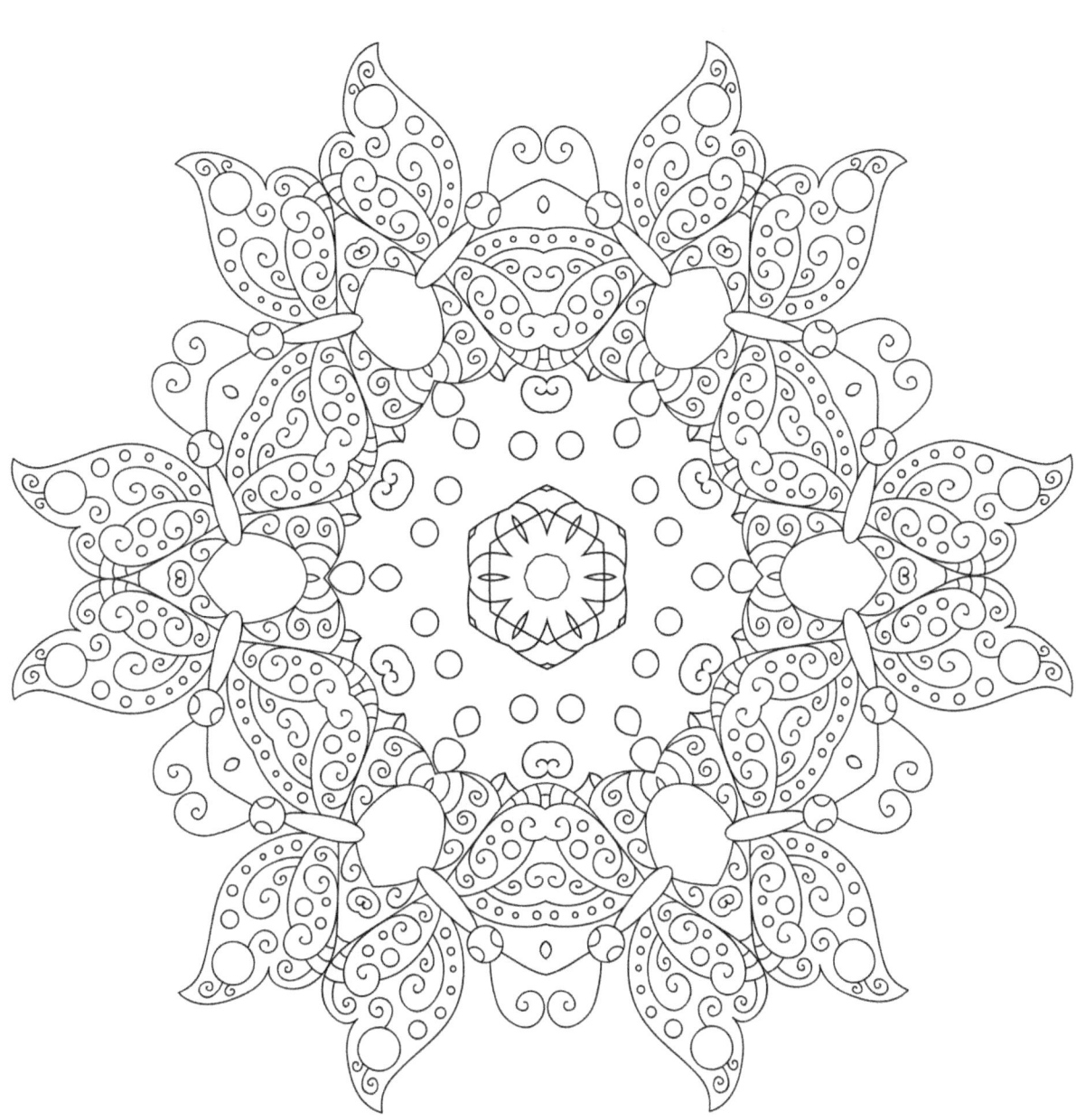

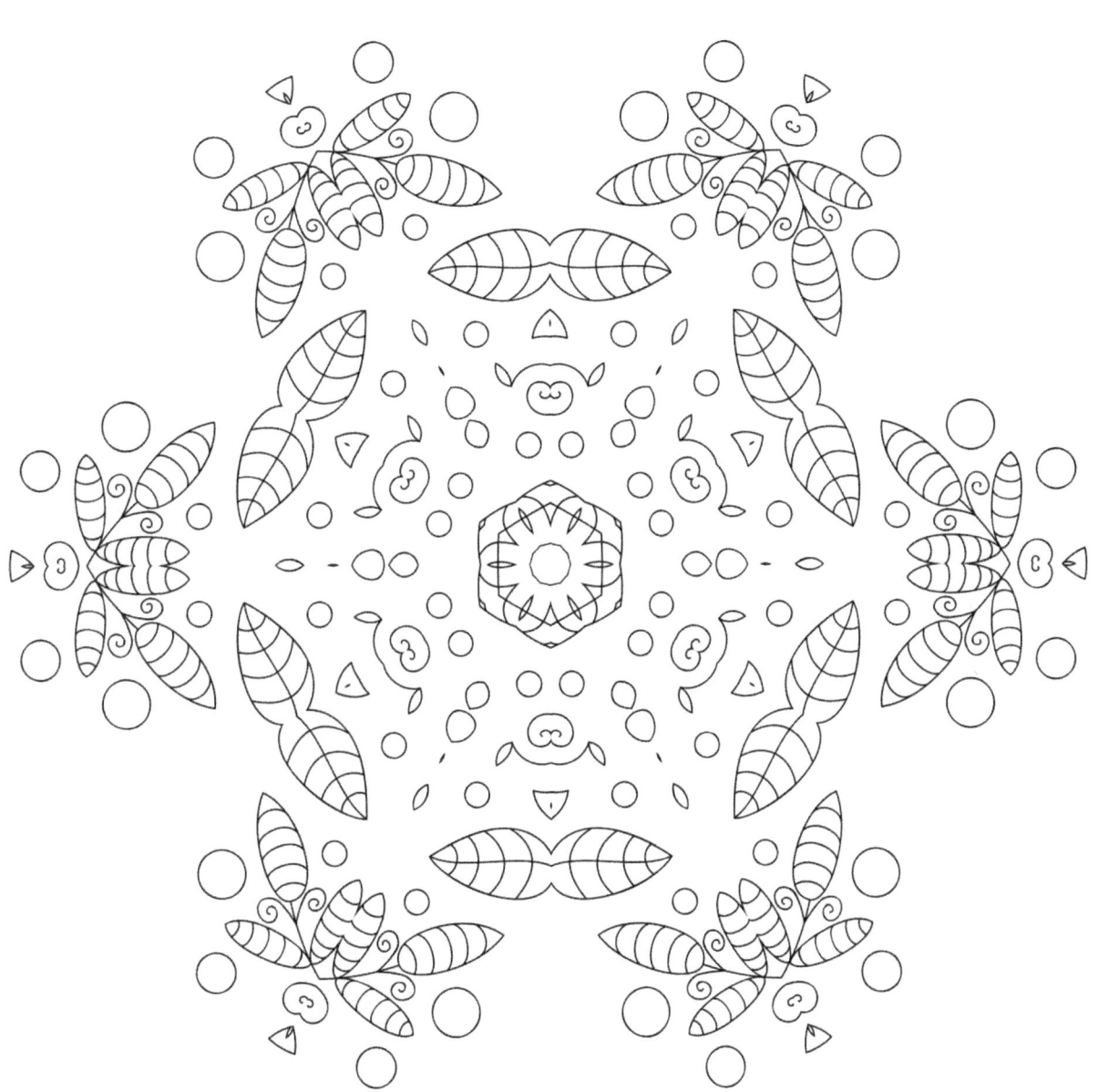

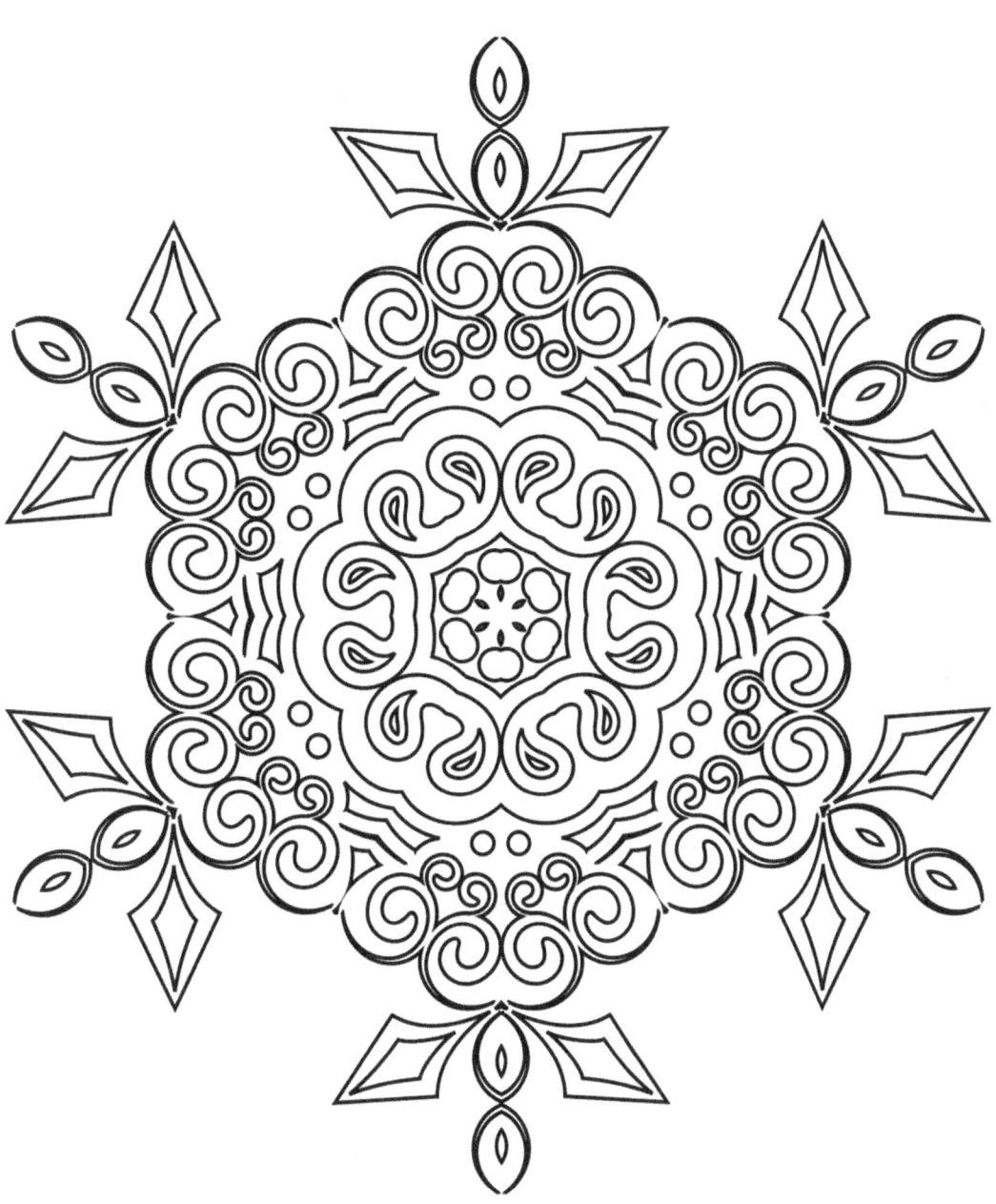

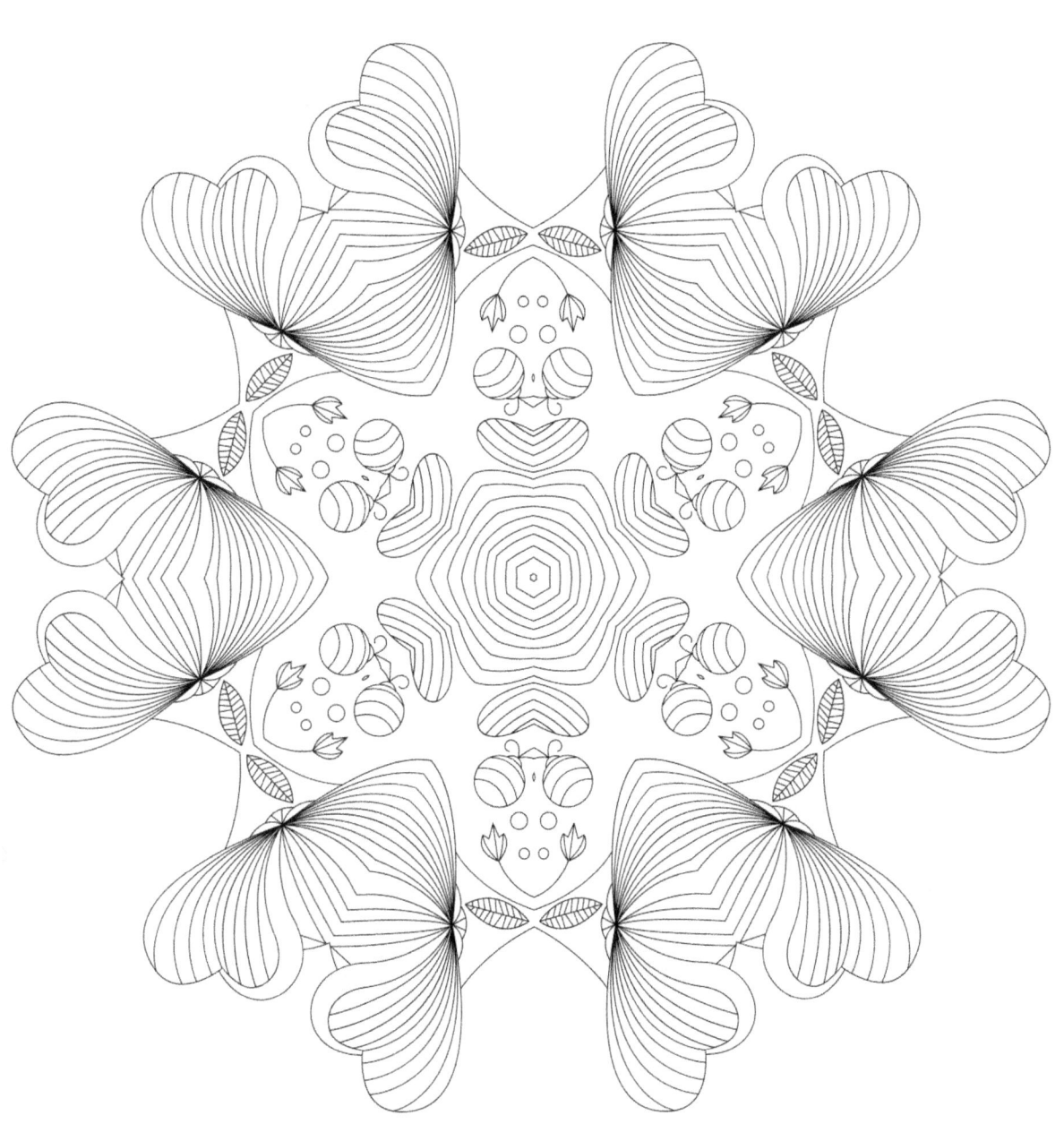

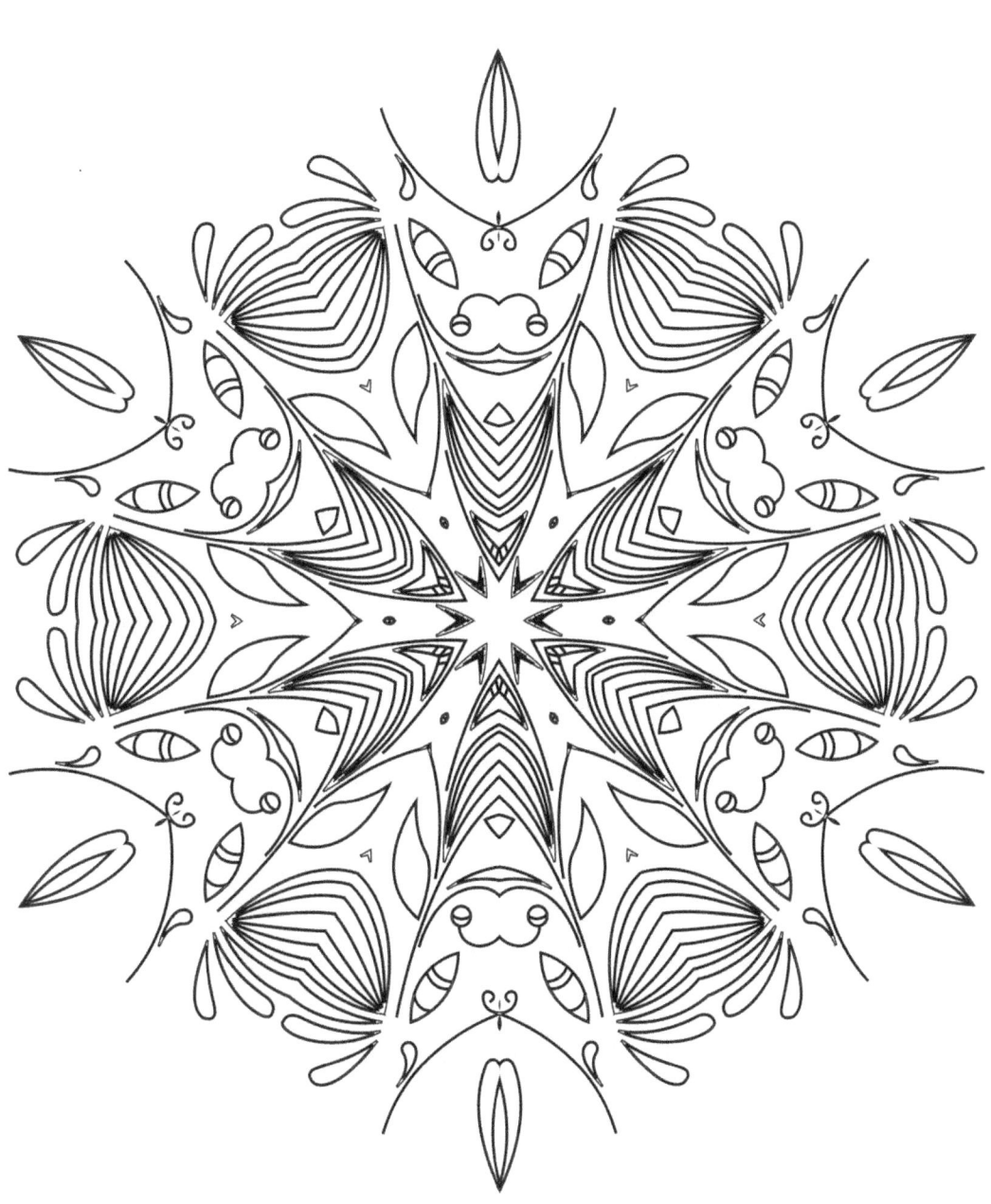

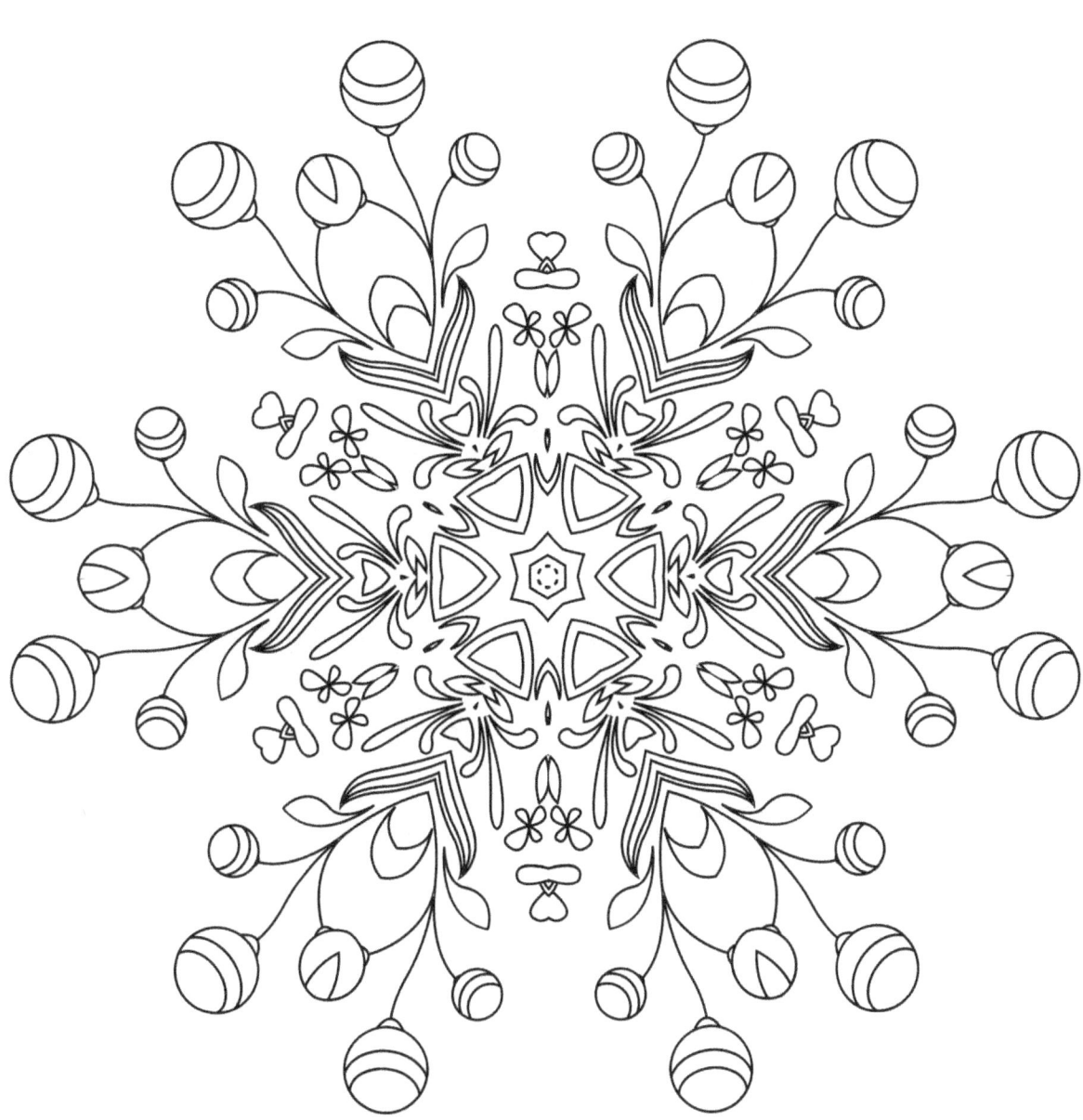

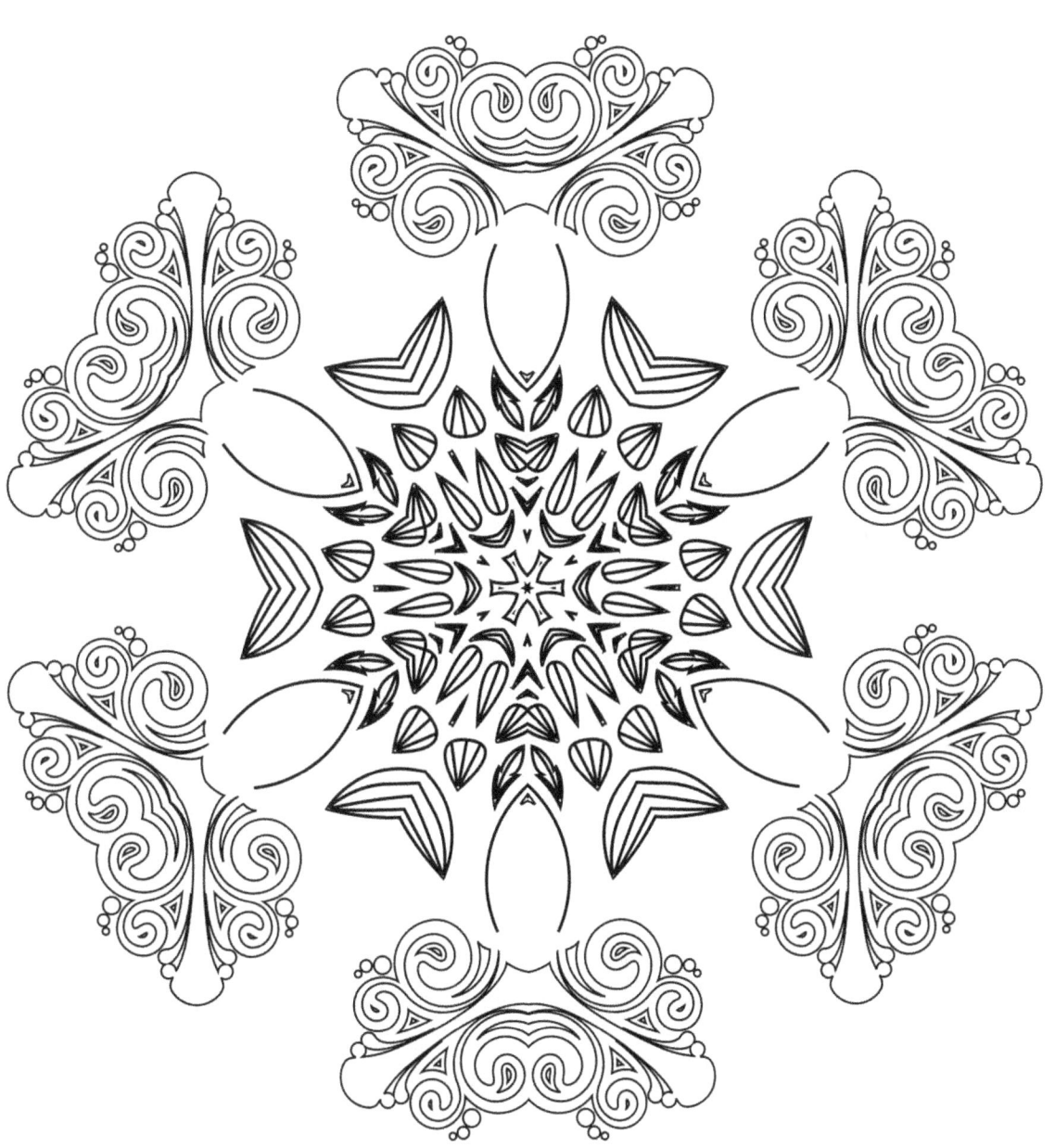

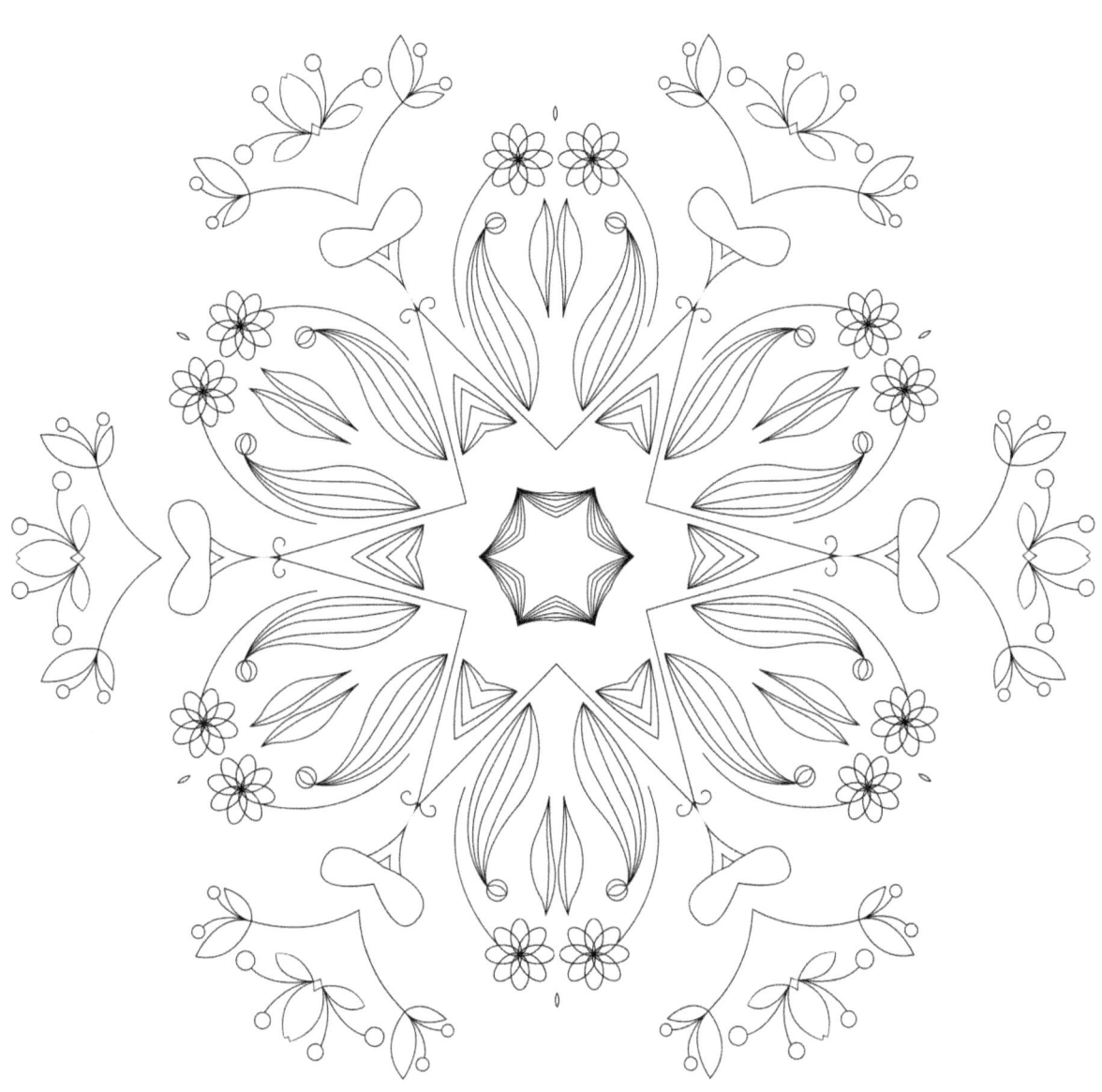

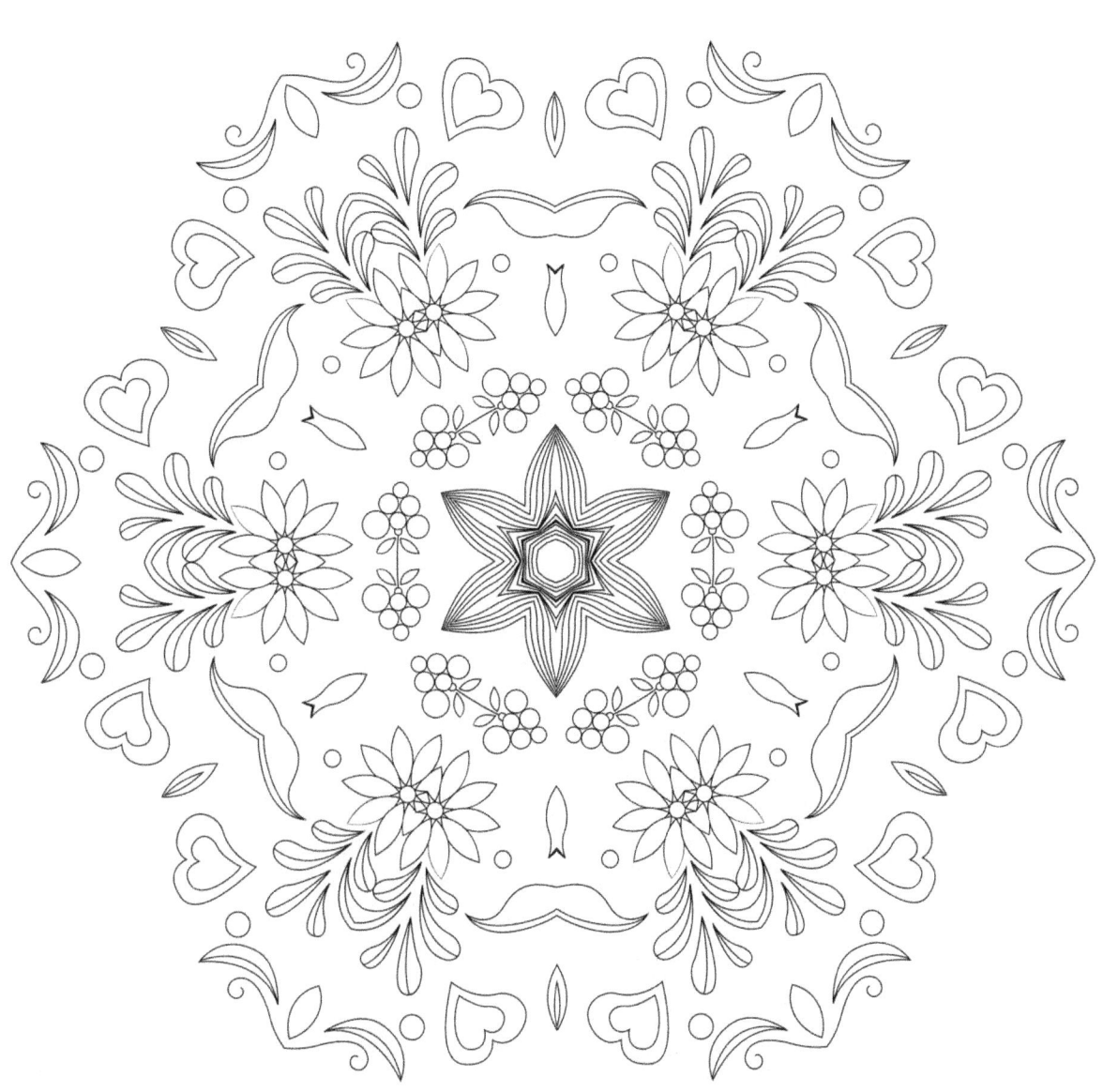

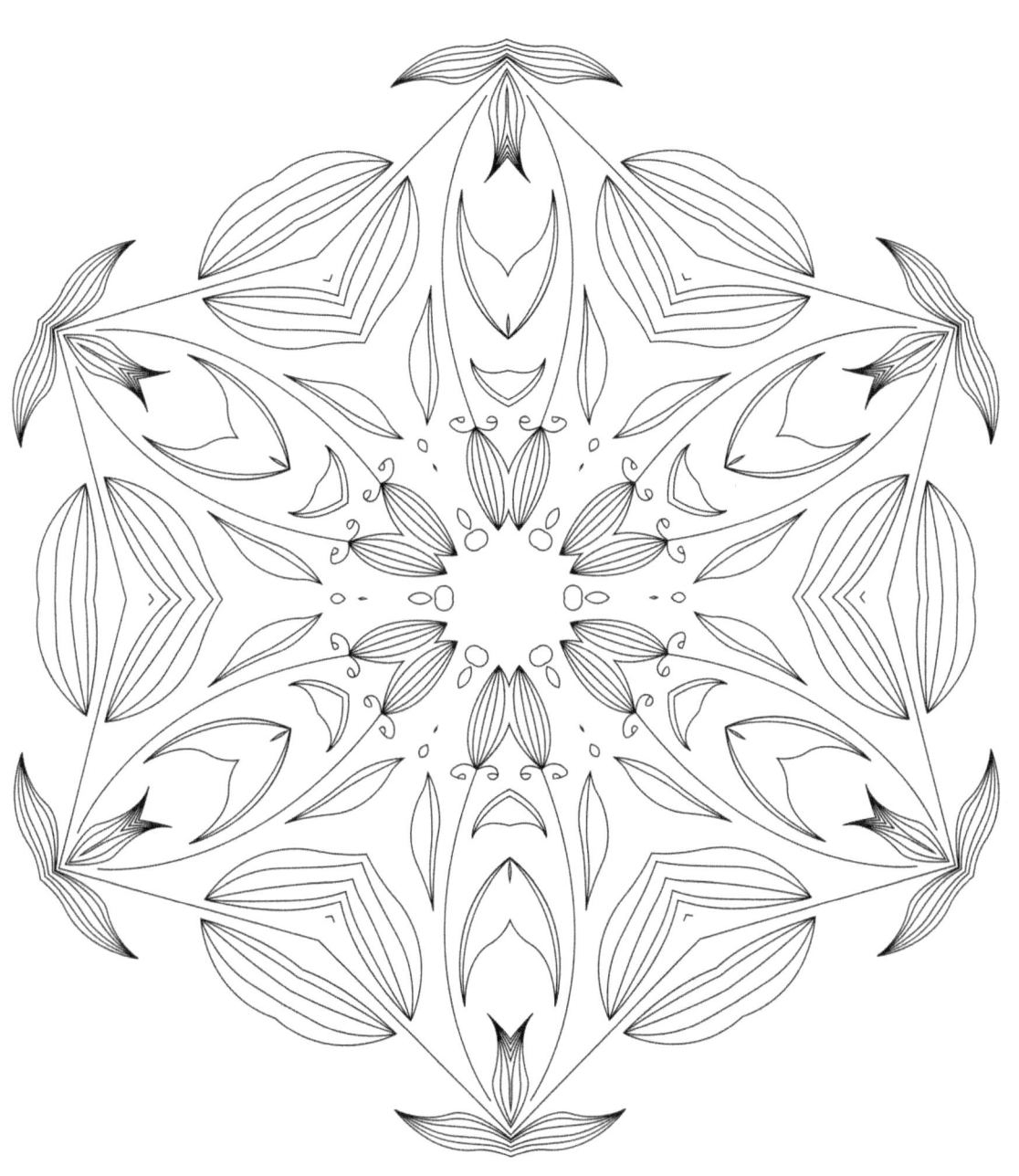

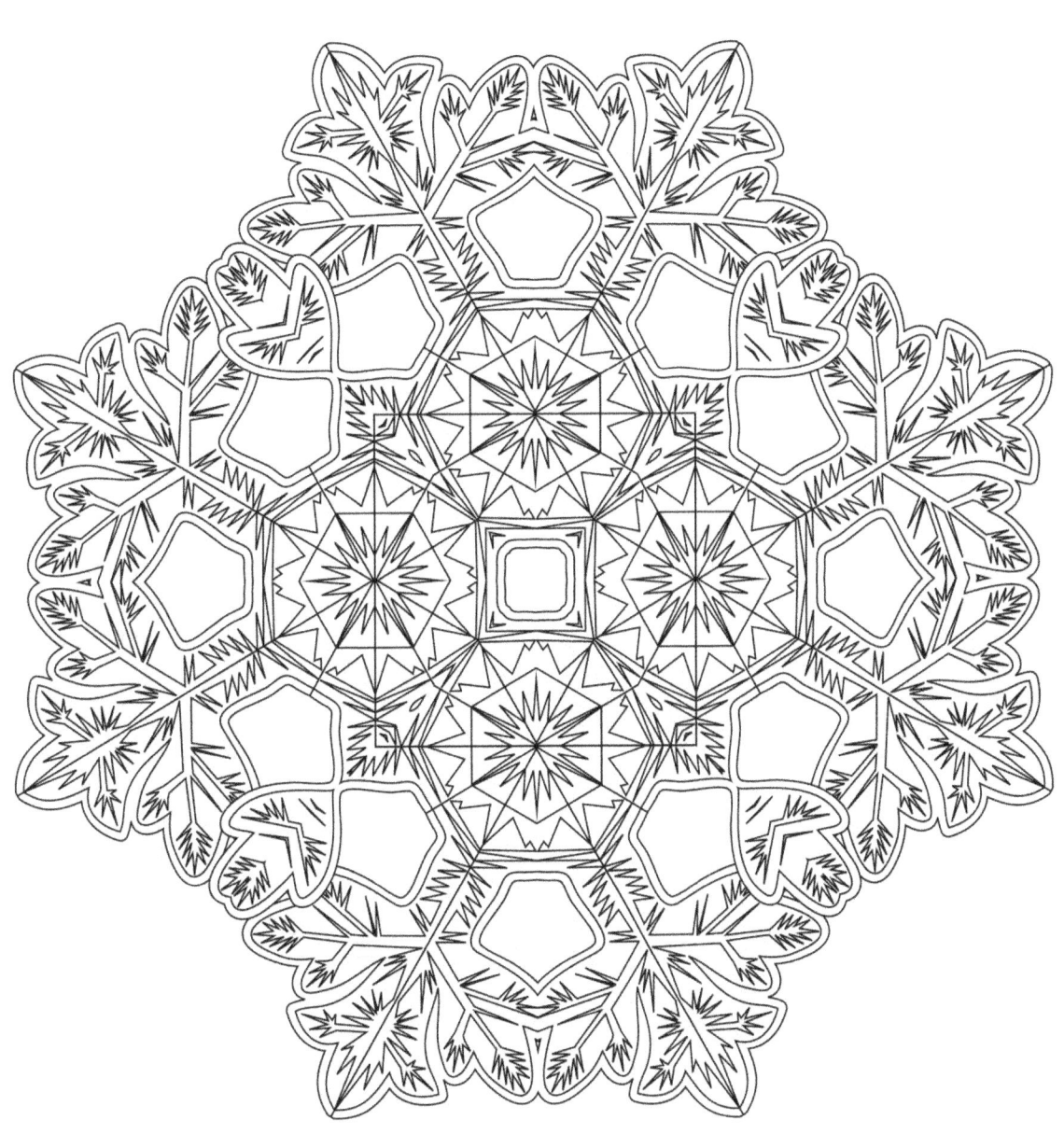

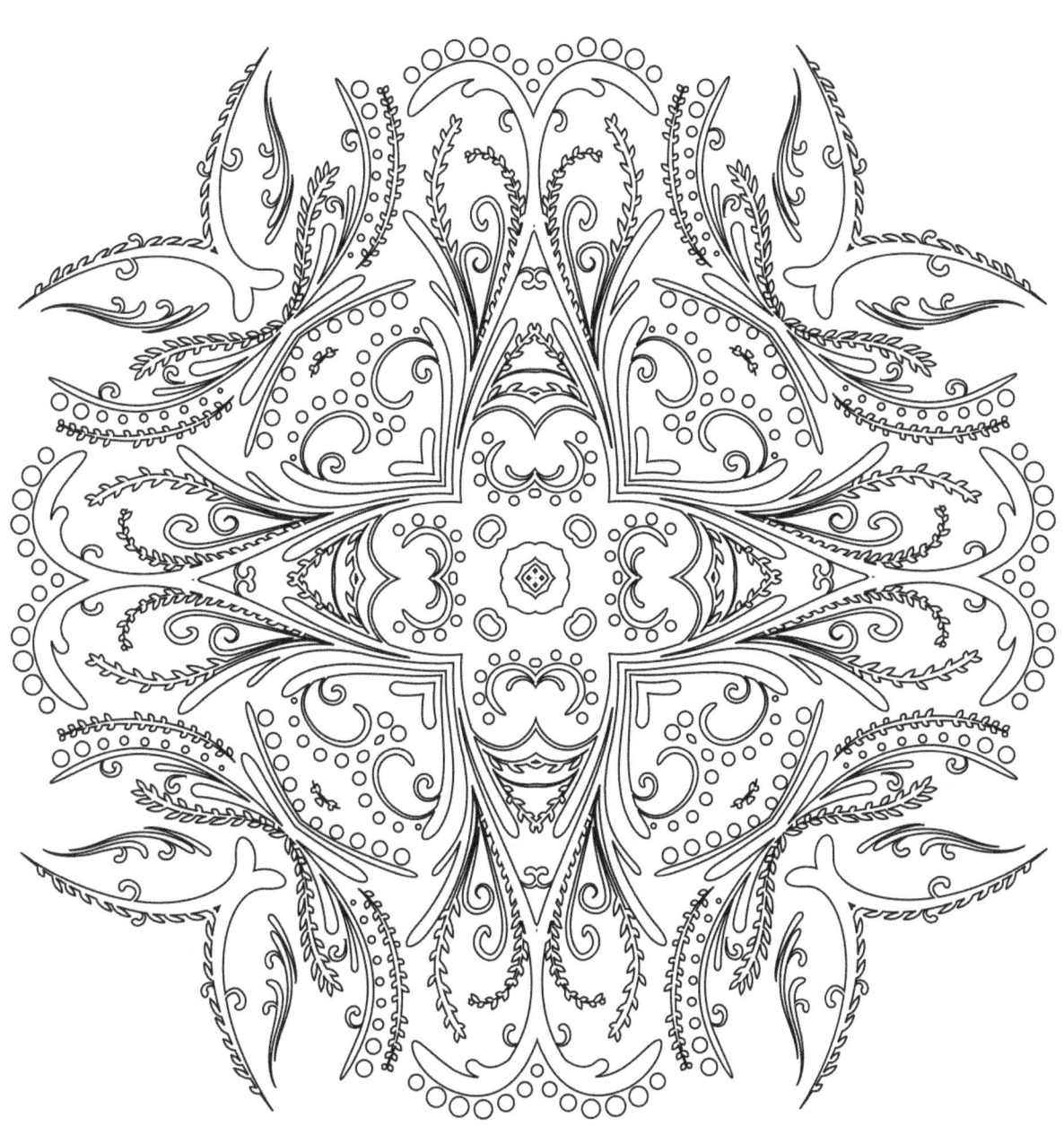

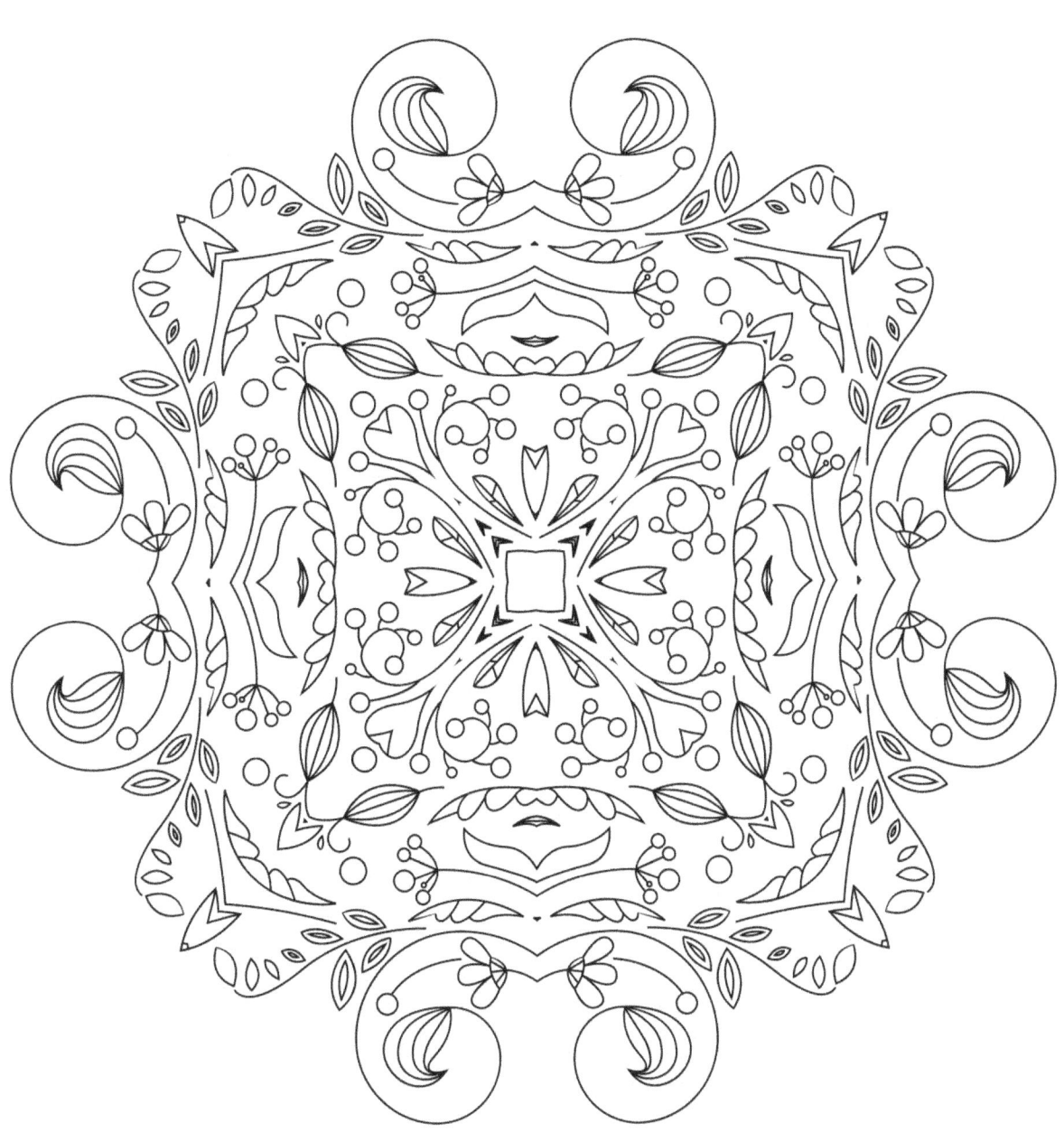

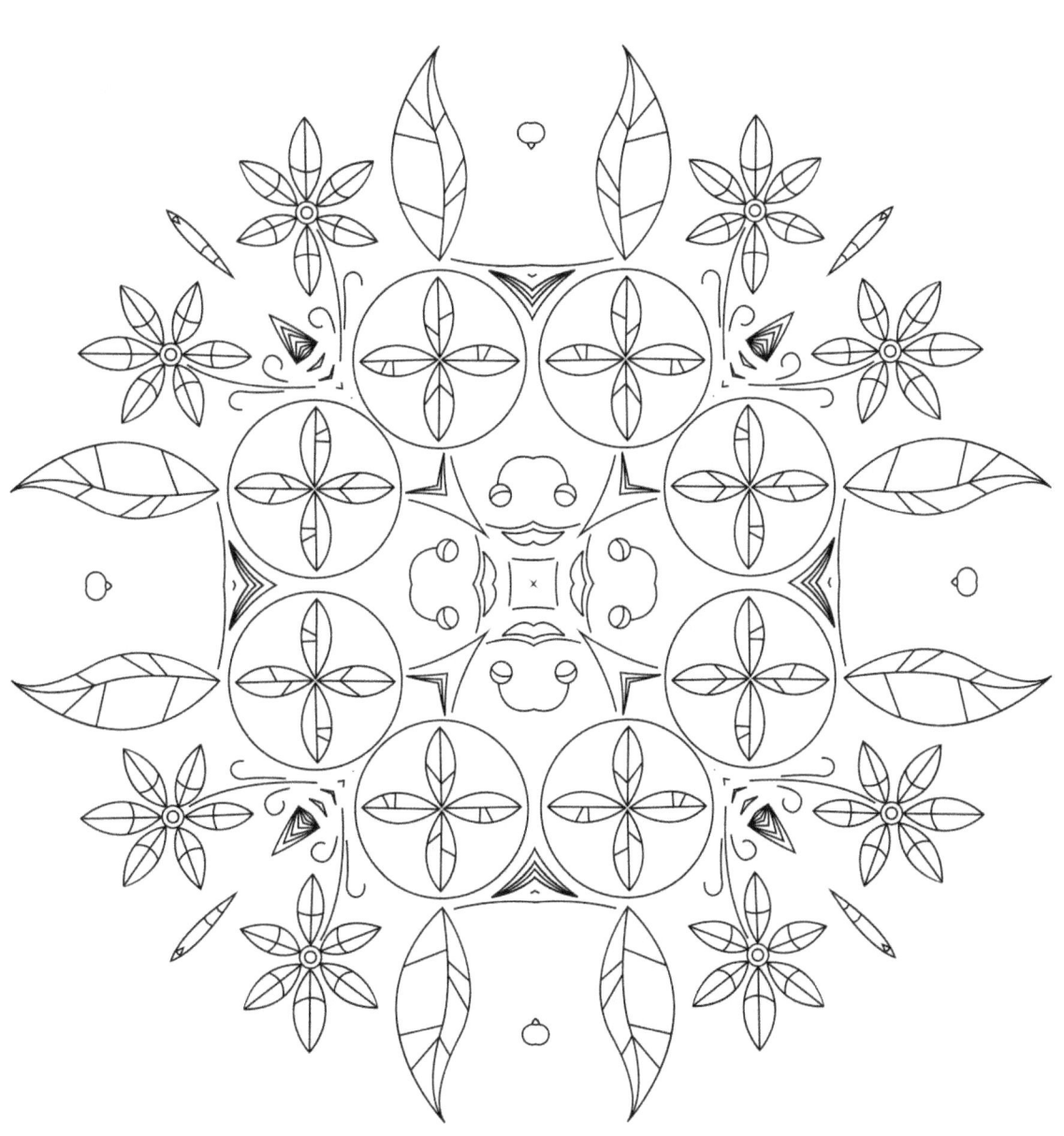

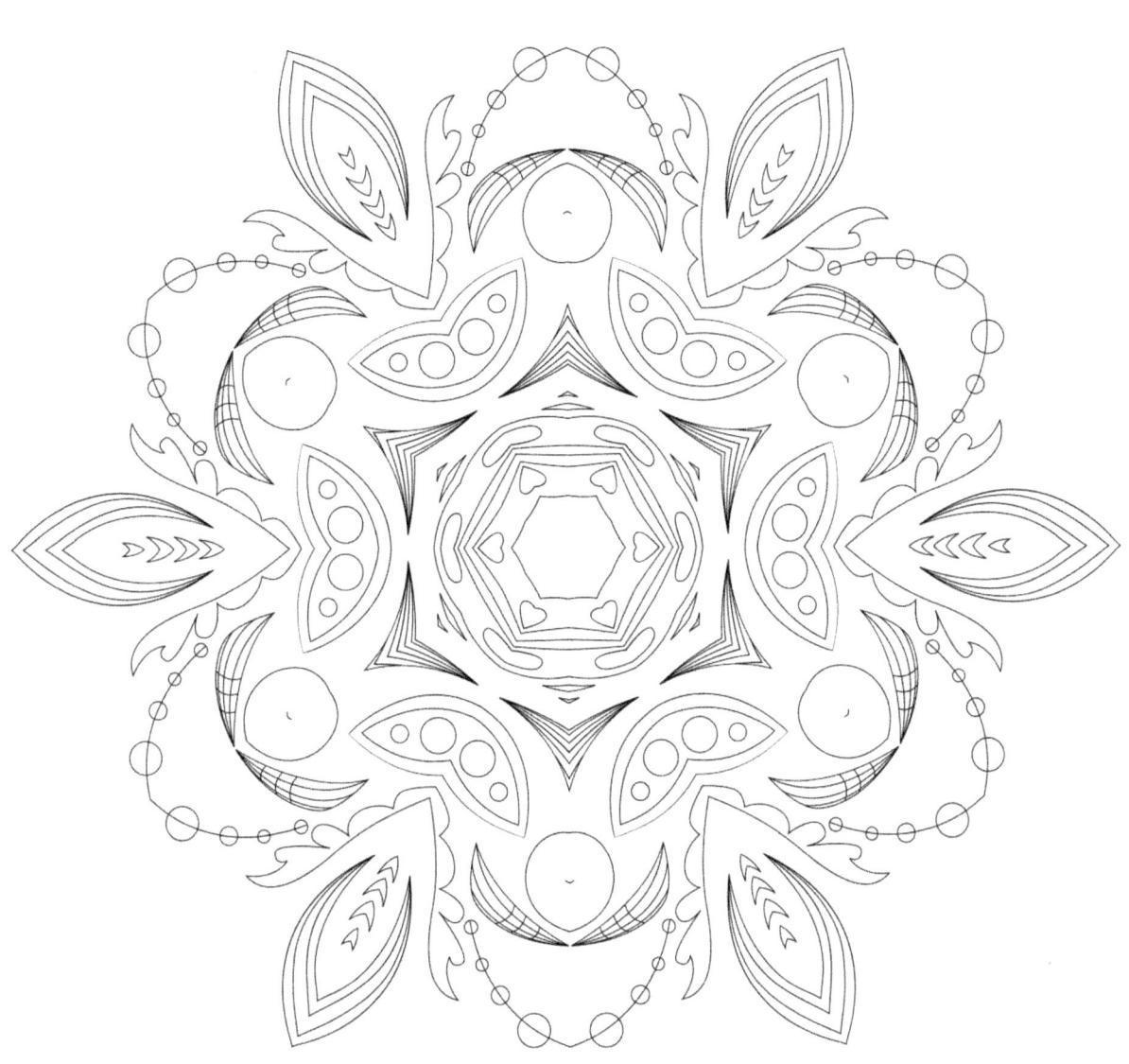

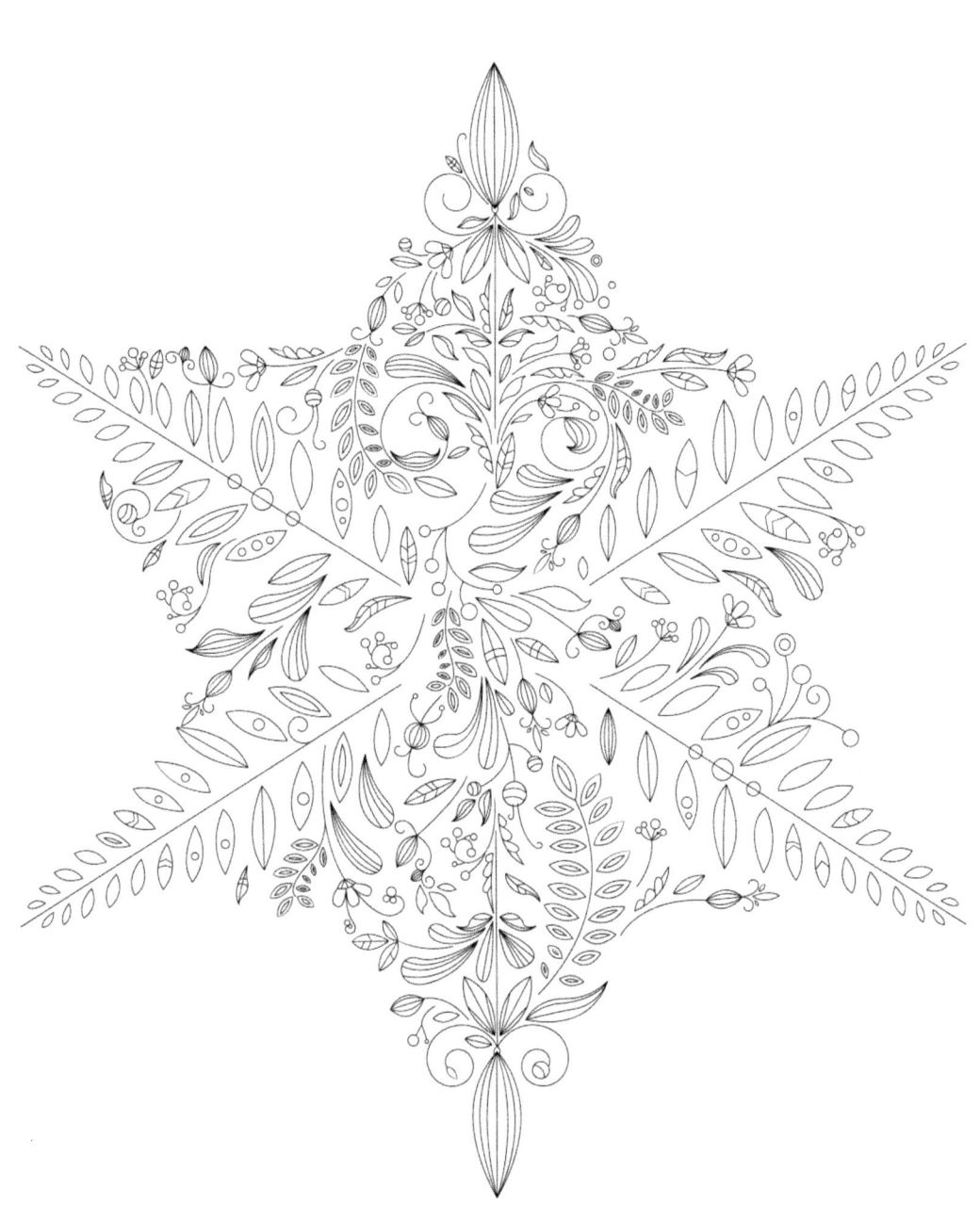

www.ingramcontent.com/pod-product-compliance
Lightning Source LLC
Chambersburg PA
CBHW081753280526
45789CB00008B/2843